EXPLORING THE SECRETES OF KINGDOM WEALTH AND PROSPERITY

(Examining the Power of Generosity)

Joseph E. Monshum

SOUL'S SEARCH PUBLICATIONS

ISBN-13: 9781234567890
ISBN-10: 1477123456

Cover design by: Art Painter
Library of Congress Control Number: 2018675309
Printed in the United States of America

CONTENTS

EXPLORING THE SECRETS OF KINGDOM WEALTH AND PROSPERITY

(Examining the Power of Generosity)

JOSEPH E. MONSHUM

DEDICATION

This book is dedicated to the end-time glorious church to

be positioned for the manifestation of kingdom wealth and prosperity on the earth. God wants to show the dying world how much He is rich, blessed and wealthy through us His sons and daughters because this are the days of His jewelries before the return of the King, the Lord Jesus for the rapture and His millennium reign.

CHAPTER ONE
GOD LOVES A CHEERFUL GIVER

God loves a cheerful giver and men also. The attitude and motives behind giving should be delightsome and cheerful to attract abundance. Cheerful is another word for having a good, bright, pleasant, glad, cheery and buoyant motive and approach in doing something, mostly in giving.

A person's attitude or conduct is always displayed or revealed when it comes to giving, whether he or she will remain cheerful, or sullen, depressing, gloomy or sad.

But according to scripture, the only attitude or motive behind giving that could attract a corresponding reward system is only when one remain cheerful or happy in giving, whereupon, such attitude attracts the grace of abundance and all-round sufficiency. "Let each one [give] as he has made up his own mind and purposed in his heart, not reluctantly or sorrowfully or under compulsion, for God loves (He takes pleasure in, prizes above other things, and is unwilling to abandon or to do without) a cheerful (joyous, "prompt to do it") giver [whose heart is in his giving] 2nd Cor. 9:7AMPC.

Giving is an act of obedience to the word of God and love for God whereupon we gain access into the miracle of abundance. When you receive the Word about prosperity and finances, it is important to back it up with corresponding action and without taking action, your financial situation may remain the same, for instance in 2nd Cor. 8:7Niv says; "But just as you excel in everything—in faith, in speech, in knowledge, in complete earnestness and in your love for us—see that you excel in this grace of giving." When you act in faith by obedient in this word just read, you position yourself to experience the miraculous blessings of the Word.

As recorded in the previous scriptures, let our giving not be in reluctance or sorrow of heart or out of necessity, neither should it be under any compulsion nor pressure but should be done cheerfully or prompt to do it as you've purposed or determined in the heart.

Let your joy and affection be in your giving and not necessarily what will return back to you. Giving should be a way or culture of life to be lived daily, since giving is living.

You see, when you have the kingdom of God as a priority, giving will now be a delight. Remember that whatever you are currently doing with your finances, especially in relation to God, to the propagation of the gospel and the advancement of the kingdom is a reflection of what you would do if your finances were multiplied a hundred times.

Someone might think, 'only if I could get a million dollar or millions of naira in my account. I will be a big financier of the kingdom of God.' The question is, have you been faithful with the little committed to you? Have you put that little in your trust into the gospel?

The lord Jesus, in Luke 16:10-11AMPC, emphasizes the principle of faithfulness and integrity in managing worldly possession when He said, "He who is faithful in a very little [thing] is faithful also in much, and he who is dishonest and unjust in a very little [thing] is dishonest and unjust also in much. Therefore if you have not been faithful in the [case of] unrighteous mammon (deceitful riches, money, possessions), who will entrust to you the true riches?"

As I said earlier that God is looking for selfless sons and daughters of His to commit and lavish His kingdom wealth and riches through them for the furtherance of the His kingdom interest on earth which is the salvation of all souls through the gospel of the kingdom.

Money is an amplifier, as in it has the unique ability to amplify, magnify or reveal one's character or conduct or even personality. Every action and decision you make with your money today is a testament, photograph or photocopy to your character, and this fundamental aspect of your character will not change when your financial resources or capacity are increased. You will simply do more of what you have been doing of either being a selfish or cheerful giver.

For people who already use their money in negative ways, having more financial resources will only amplify those negative actions. Reversibly, if you're using your money for righteous purpose, seeding the gospel, and advancing the interest of the kingdom, having more money will amplify those good actions.

That is why you need to examine your current financial behaviours; do they align with the principles of God's word? God is pleased to multiply the finances of those who are committed to His righteous cause of seeding the gospel and helping the poor.

When you prioritize serving the Lord and His kingdom's interest, your actions with money become a testament or photocopy of your faithfulness. It's not about the amount of money you possess; rather, it's the alignment of your heart and intension with God's purpose.

Nevertheless, by consistently prioritizing the Gospel of Jesus Christ and seeking His Kingdom above all else, you position yourself to experience God's provisions and the abundance of your resources being a cheerful giver. "so above all, constantly seek God's kingdom and his righteousness, then all these less important things will be given to you abundantly." Matt. 6:33 TPT.

CHAPTER TWO

EXCEED THE LAW OF TIGHTING

The New Testament church is not restricted to laws, even the law of tithing but we are admonished to be generous in giving, as in giving above your tithing capacity. The law was giving to Moses by angels, Moses being the mediator, Gal. 3:19.

The original plan of God for man was not to operate under any law from the onset. It's because God from the origin had intended to operate a family system and a kingdom of priests, holy and peculiar through which He can relate with humankind in fellowship, partnership and friendship.

In the account of Exodus from the nineteenth chapter, they detested that offer of the Fatherhood of God and chose to serve to be rebellious like other nations, whereupon God have to hand them over to be tutored by angels through laws wherein Moses was their mediator from chapter twenty of Exodus.

Ordinarily, laws are meant for servants and not sons in the house. Angels are ruled by the law of justice, equity and fairness which they used the same approach to tutor the children of Israel and any defaulter was given a due recompense or punishment, even death, since the strength of sin is the law and the strength of the law is death.

The Old Testament law is the laws of restrictions filled with 'do's' and 'don'ts' while the new testament law is rules by liberty. The old produces death while the new produces life, and even life eternal.

The Old Testament laws are driven by fear and death since it gave strength to sin and guilt and the New Testament laws are driven by faith and life, since it gave strength to righteousness and assurance or boldness forevermore.

The reason why I brought this little analogy is because "for the law was given by Moses, but grace and truth came by Jesus Christ." John 1:17kjv. And we are not under the Law of Moses motivated by restrictions and punishments for its defaulters but we are under the law of Christ which is grace and truth or liberty and life.

Don't take tithe as a law nor kingdom tax since both are driven out of necessity, fear of defaulting and a kind of compulsion, rather take tithe as a sense or response or token of appreciation for the bountifulness and benevolence of God towards you with the motive of worship and thanksgiving, knowing also that such practice is the foundation of your prosperity and the starting point of your generosity that connects you to His overflowing blessings of abundance.

Now, you will say that if I am against tithing then why Abraham did paid tithe, and that period was not the dispensation of the law. Abraham did not pay tithe but gave the tithe of all he had. "And blessed be the most high God, which hath delivered thine enemies into thy hand. And he **gave** him tithe of all" Gen. 14:20kjv. (Emphasis mine).

This is the point I am bringing here that there is a difference between paying and giving. Paying involves obligation, necessity, compulsion, tasking, sorrow of heart and force, while giving involves willingness, responsibility, cheerfulness, generosity, liberty or liberality and joy.

Abraham operated under the law of liberty which was grace, and gave generously even to the extent of giving his only son, since He was love or worship driven and not necessarily as an obligation.

God operates in a monarchy kind of kingdom or governing system where the King or Monarch is solely responsible for the welfare of its citizens and enjoys seeing the prosperity of His citizens since it reflects the wealth or glory of His kingdom and image.

God is not looking for anyone to assist Him with anything because the silver and gold are His Hag. 2:8, and the earth is His and the fullness thereof Ps. 24:1. He cannot task any because it is an insult to His benevolence. But He loves our giving generously as a reflection of His character or nature inbuilt in us which gives Him glory or pleasure that we resemble Him, since it is a Kingdom of givers and selfless in nature and not accumulators and selfish system which is the reflection of the fallen human kingdom.

The church now have come into a place of transaction in the matter of tithing and when the desired result is not reached, they become offended with God that He isn't fair to His Word in opening the windows of heaven and shower the blessing. Now the motive of giving become wrong based on transaction and not love or kingdom motivated.

When you read closely in the book of Malachi the primary purpose of tithing, was to make meat available in the house of God to sustain the priests which was a kingdom dream Mal. 3:10. But in the body of Christ today, we are more interested in the blessings and are not driven by the kingdom to care for the house of God as our motive that is driven by worship and love, rather our hearts now is only in the blessing aspect of our freedom from the devourers and the windows of heaven opened.

There we miss it, and the reason why many don't experience the blessings of the kingdom is due to our wrong seeking. "But seek ye first the kingdom of God, and his righteousness; and all these things shall be added unto you" Matt. 6:33. This is the secret of the prosperity of Bishop Oyedepo of Living Faith church.

One certain day when I was meditating on that Mal. Chapter three, about tithing, the Lord told me that tithe which is one tenth of all our earnings is the extent of man's selfishness and the best of his generosity. That is, if anyone could freely and generously give his or her tithe, you immediately receive freedom from selfishness that engrossed the fallen Man, Adam, since that is the best he could do, pertaining giving.

I am talking of the fallen Man as in the first Adam who is a living soul. But we are of the last Adam who is a quickening spirit; thereupon we should do better not in selfishness or percentage but more generously above the ten percent which is the best of the fallen man's generosity of what he can easily spare.

When you are still struggling to even give the ten percent, then you are not ready for financial overflow because it takes selflessness to access the abundance of creation which your faithfulness in tithing could handle naturally, and when you exceed that percentage, you start experiencing a running over financial blessing, for there are no substitutes or options for this truth.

When the natural man is born of God, he or she become selfless and giving now becomes a delight since the motive is now right and different as they see giving as a sense of worship and also driving the interest of the kingdom, they give generously as a responsibility not as an obligation or necessity to keep or transaction to make with God, since they have this mentality that they are already blessed with all spiritual and earthly blessings and all things are theirs by redemption, 2nd Pet. 1:3, 1st Cor. 3:21 and Eph. 1:3.

I know of several believers who give more than just ten percent of their earnings up to ninety percent of their earnings and they are living in abundance since they take giving not as a transaction but as kingdom promoters and all other things with the windows and even doors of heaven is added to them due to their generosity.

The moment you develop the power to give there will be a corresponding power to receive back in abundance because no one can out give God. "But this I say, He which soweth sparingly shall reap also sparingly; and he which soweth bountifully shall also rap bountifully. Every man according as he purposeth in his heart, so let him give, not grudgingly, or of necessity: for God loveth a cheerful giver." 2nd Cor. 9:6-7kjv.

These are all kingdom principles that can never be neglected in order not to suffer material deficit on the earth or connecting to the abundance of God's riches or material wealth on earth naturally because the kingdom system is understanding both the person and principle of Christ, whereupon the person of Christ makes you qualified to inherit His eternal kingdom forever but His principles grants you access to enjoy the good of the earth, which one of the principles is to tithe and exceed the laws of tithing and start giving generously to enjoy the abundance of the earth and be positioned to be one of the distributors of the wealth of heaven in this last days.

CHAPTER THREE
CONQUERING THE INFLUENCE OF GREED

The moment giving becomes a delight or a way of life without any sense of compulsion or necessity but liberal and cheerful finding joy and much excitement in your giving, is an indication that you have conquered greed and simultaneously connected into abundance. Poverty and lack is when you are afraid to give.

Nonetheless, poverty in this context is lack and want, but the true sense of poverty is more of spiritual than physical limitations which is the absent of peace, joy and righteousness, the absence of the kingdom of God in the heart of man is poverty. When one's sin remains and there is no peace or joy, but guilt and fear in such a soul no matter the abundance of physical substance, he or she is still poor and in abject poverty.

Show me a poor man or a woman of lack and wants, I will show you a man or woman that is afraid of giving or self-centered and does not love giving, but always loves receiving. When one is afraid to give either substance or cash is an indication that greed still has a very strong influence over such fellow.

The human life is a makeup of greed and lies, while the divine life of God is a makeup of grace and truth. "For the law was give by Moses, but grace and truth came by Jesus Christ" John 1:17kjv. Grace which is the lifestyle or character of truth is the component of the divine life while greed which is the lifestyle or character of lies is the components of the human life.

For anyone to conquer the influence of greed, they must be an upgrade from operating within the human realm of life into the divine or God-kind of life which is eternal life, whereupon giving generously becomes a delight because the nature of God is consistent in giving since it is always love driven. "For God so loved the world, that he gave his only begotten son…" John 3:16a and we that operates in this class of life ought to be generous givers also, "Hereby perceive we the love of God, because he laid down his life for us: and we ought to lay down our lives for the brethren." 1st John 3:16kjv.

Giving generously for emphasis is an indication that you have conquered greed, and you are simultaneously connected to the grace of abundance whereupon you begin to experience the wealth of heaven on earth naturally without stress or strain.

"But this I say, He which soweth sparingly shall reap also sparingly; and he which soweth bountifully shall reap also bountifully. Every man according as he purposeth in his heart, so let him give; not grudgingly, or of necessity: for God loveth a cheerful giver. And God is able to make all grace abound toward you; that ye, always having all sufficiency in all things, may abound to every good work: (As it is written, He hath dispersed abroad, he hath given to the poor: his righteousness remaineth for ever." 2nd Cor. 9:6-9kjv.

I love the rendition of the amplified version in vs. eight of the above scripture. "And God is able to make all grace (every favor and earthly blessing) come to you in abundance, so that you may always and under all circumstances and whatever the need be self-sufficient [possessing enough to require no aid or support and furnished for every good work and charitable donation]" 2nd Cor. 9:8AMPC.

When greed is conquered through giving, grace abounds, attracting every favor and earthly blessing in abundance, possessing enough to require no aid or support and decked for always ever ready for every good work and charitable donations.

What a triumphant kind of life that is lived when greed is

conquered through generous giving, you become a distributor of God's resources or wealth on earth. You start experiencing prosperity of satisfactory progress in all your earthly endeavors and able to distribute to others in need. Remember that silver and gold are His, Haggai 2:8.

I have come to fully understand that when one is greedy he or she is at the same time selfish and self-centered and will always be afraid to give, and when you are afraid to give, you are poor as iterated above, no matter the volume of wealth or riches in your possession.

All this truth is connected to natural laws or the laws that govern nature or cause and effects or sowing and reaping. I met a lady who told me that she always love sharing all that she had and have never run broke before, even to the extent that whenever she is in need of a million naira, it answers to her desire within a very short space of time as a gift.

The day I met with her she paid my transport fair and even left the left over balance for the driver because scripturally, "There is that scattereth, and yet increaseth; and there is that withholdeth more than is meet, but it tendeth to poverty" Prov. 11:24. The good news bible rendition of this verse is so interesting, "Some people spend their money freely and still grow richer. Others are cautious, and yet grow poor" Prov. 11:24, GNBDK.

God in this last days is looking for His sons and daughters that have conquered the influenced of greed through their generosity so that He can lavish His kingdom wealth and riches through them for the purpose of the propagation of the gospel on earth and the support of the weak that cannot afford anything for themselves.

Let's move on to unveiling the next chapter where we shall be dealing with the channels through which one could always give generously as a lifestyle with all delight.

CHAPTER FOUR
EXPLORING THE CHANNELS OF GIVING

Giving is living, the moment one stops giving, death is inevitable. The deaths are of dissatisfaction, stagnation, non-fulfillment, non-excitement, worries, anxieties and confusion. These sinister kinds of death are far worse than the physical death when the soul departs from the body which the live of giving can prevent, cure or be an arsenal.

We shall begin to explore scripturally the channels through which we could engage our giving to maximize our living on the earth.

THE CHANNELS OF KINGDOM GIVING

1. **SEED SOWING:** "While the earth remaineth, seedtime and harvest and cold and heat, and day and night shall not cease." Gen. 8:22. When I was going through this scripture, I discovered that sowing any seed always have a time or season in doing it, but harvest has no specific time or season to reap the reward of the seed sown.

Seed sowing is giving what we have or what you've got in exchange by trust in God for what you want or desire, it is a supernatural value exchange rate system of giving what is less in your best possible for what is more to your surprise. I also discovered that seed sowing is a law that governs the entire universe related to the law of cause and effects and sowing and reaping. Before commanding any tangible and visible effects in the natural, there must be a causal effect, nothing just happens without a cause, (work) or favor.

Always have this understanding that seed sowing is not

burdensome because it is God that supplies seed to the one that sows and bread to the eaters. "(as it is written, he that dispersed abroad; he hath given to the poor: his righteousness remaineth for ever. Now he that ministereth seed to the sower both minister bread for your food, and multiply your seed sown and increase the fruits of your righteousness.)" And also in Isaiah 55:10 "… that it may give seed to the sower, and bread to the eater" talking about the rain of blessing. The moment your heart is made up to sow into the kingdom it is dramatically made available in your hands.

One can sow finances, manual services, and specialized or professional service seed for the purpose of the less privilege or common good and the gospel of Christ, the returns is always amazing.

One day God told me that, for all of my desire in prayer, I should make it a habit of sowing either financial or service seed to be properly positioned to receive what I want with ease and actually it is working. It is the power of faith expression.

Whenever I pray or prophesy for a need, the next thing I do is to abound in thanksgiving as though I have received it and finally I sow seed of service or finance to build up my confidence of receiving what I have already asked for.

Seeds sowing could be done several times in several places since it is good to cast your bread unto many waters, and you may not know the one that may rise after many days as a reward system for you. See. Eccl. 11:1-2.

Every good you do to someone or to the work of the gospel, is seed sowing and you should always expect a reward in return as you do it generously.

2. **TITHES AND OFFERINGS;** This is one of the kingdom ways of investment, life naturally was given for investment and not just to be spent, the moment you

invest your life on profitable ventures, you emerge an asset, but when life is only spent on pleasure and unprofitable ventures, you end up a liability, this also applies to your finances. Well, most people do say that we should not expect something back from God by making our tithe and offering as money producing machine with God to meet up our financial quest, that it should be given out of love. They are right in some extent because I think the motive behind your giving really matters which have been treated in the previous chapter that our motive primarily should be in pursuit of kingdom dream which is for the work the gospel, the poor and the His ministers.

When giving your tithe which is ten percent or one tenth of all your earnings or since we are not under the law now, but grace, it could be twenty percent or more in the expression of your love and generosity with God. One of the laws of life is that when we give anything; it comes back to us good measures press down running together shall men give to your boson. Luke. 6:38.

But giving is first of all the expression of our love and gratitude for God and secondly it is the expression of the abundance we have in Christ, so we don't give to make us rich, we are already rich and blessed and is made manifest in the physical as material wealth, health, peace, strength etc through our practical involvement in our cheerful giving. "Will a man rob God? Yet ye have robbed me. But ye say, Wherein have we robbed thee? In tithes and offerings" Mal.3:8.

Those that responds to this instructions get all the blessings manifesting in their lives from the store house of heaven until there will be no place to store them—abundance!

    3. PROPHETIC OFFERINGS; By our redemption in Christ, we share in the prophetic, kingly and priestly anointing, but there is a prophetic office whereupon one could be called to function for the perfecting of the saints in the work of the ministry, for the edifying of the body of Christ onto the fullness of the stature of Christ. See Eph. 4:11-13. Any prophet that is received in the name of a prophet shall also receive a prophetic reward which is prosperity, since he is believed because you cannot receive one that you have not believed.

Genuine prosperity comes from when a prophet is received, believed and held with honor, and then you enjoy all that the prophet carries. "… He that receiveth a prophet in the name of a prophet shall receive a prophet's reward;" Matt. 10:41a. The prophet is the major custodian of prosperity to the saints and God could only establish you, but proper you by the hand or ministry of a prophet. Most folks don't honor their prophets but believes in the Lord and don't prosper and wonder why. "…Believe in the Lord your God, so shall ye be established; believe his prophets, so shall ye prosper" 2nd Cor. 20:20.

4. **GIVING TO THE POOR;** This is one of the kingdom ways of investment, since any one that gives to the poor lends to the Lord and He will pay back what you gave. "he that hath pity upon the poor lendeth unto the Lord; and that which he hath given will he pay him back." Prov. 19:17, and remember also that; "whoso stoppeth his ears at the cry of the poor, he also shall cry himself, but shall not be heard." Pro. 21:13, and most excitingly in Psalm 41:1-3 "BLESSED IS he that considereth the poor: the Lord will deliver him in time of trouble.

The Lord will preserve him, and keep him alive; and he shall be blessed upon the earth: and thou wilt not deliver him unto the will of his enemies. The Lord will strengthen him upon the bed of languishing: thou wilt make all his bed in his sickness". When you remember the poor, you've remembered God, and when God is remembered, you also shall be remembered at the point of your need.

5. **PROJECT OFFERINGS:** Going though the book of Exodus 36:3-7; "… And they spake unto Moses, saying, the people bring much more than enough for the service of the work, which the Lord commanded to make. For the stuff they had was sufficient for all the work to make it, and too much. Project offerings are given for the service of the physical building of the body of Christ, the schools, church building, humanitarian centers, hospitals for the common good when supported; it attracts tremendous blessings, even financially.

6. **GIVING TO PARENTS:** "But if any provide not for his own, and specially for those of his own house, he hath denied the faith, and is worse than an infidel" 1st Tim. 5:8. Giving to parents is one of the biblical strategies to immerse in wealth and mostly financial prosperity. "Honour thy father and mother; which is the first commandment with promise; That it may be well with thee, and thou mayest live long on the earth" Eph.6:2-3.

The best way to honour our parents is with our substance, and you could just imagine the blessing that follows—that it might be well with thee in your business, career, health, education etc. and on top of that, you shall be satisfied with long life. What else do we want in life more than these blessings?

The life that is well is the life free from sickness and disease with frustration and lack, but rich, satisfied and fulfilling sort of life with length of days added, that is heaven on earth experience that most times we miss out by not extending our helping hands to our parents both physical and spiritual or elderly ones in our families, even when or not we've lost our biological parents.

7. **FIRST FRUITS AND SACRIFICIAL OFFERINGS:** " Honour the Lord with thy substance, and with the first fruits of all thine increase: So shall thy barns be filled with plenty, and thy presses shall burst out with new

wine." Prov. 3:9-10. This is another kingdom ways of appreciating the goodness of God in one's life over the works of his or her hands. First fruits is the first increase of all your endeavours which was derived as a law in Exodus 22:29 "Thou shalt not delay to offer the first of thy ripe fruits, and of thy liquors: the first born of thy sons shalt thou give unto me" though as it were as a law to be observed but more so, we who are in this new dispensation of the grace of God does this with cheerfulness and as a law of faith to obtain the blessing that follows, just as God gave Christ as the first fruit of rising from the death which the old testament used as a typology in both verses read above.

Giving to God the best of its kind is first fruit which attracts exponential blessing of the same kind of fruit sown which Abel did in the accounts of Genesis, just as the resurrection of Jesus Christ brought all of us sons and daughters of God into the same glory as His children, but Christ was first given by God sacrificially as the only begotten Son of God, John, 3:16.

First fruits could be the first salary of the year given to God for the work of the gospel or to the poor either in business or carrier and also the first increase of all your earnings could be given as thanksgiving to God.

Sacrificial offering is giving whatever you are prompted to give by the Holy-Spirit or deep conviction, it is most time difficult since it is always what you desire most as in the case of Abraham our father of faith who gave his only Isaac, the son he loved for a sacrifice, which he obeyed, though God did not allow him kill the young boy, but by his obedience he became a father of many nations by just an attempt to sacrifice one child, see Gen. 22:1-18. Every sacrificial giving that is obeyed always yields a tremendous blessing that is always so fascinating to the giver.

One could sow a seed to reap a harvest correspondingly, but sacrificial giving could change a whole situation that have been pending by giving divine solutions palpable of experiencing complete restoration over expected desires.

When I was going through the gospel of Luke 6:38 which states "Give, and it shall be given unto you; good measure, pressed down, and shaken together, and running over, shall men give into your bosom. For with the same measure that ye mete withal it shall be measured to you again." Going by scriptures, the number six signifies creation going through the accounts of Genesis, and three stands for resurrection or completion while eight stands for a new beginning going through the story of Noah.

The moment we imbibe the attitude of relentless giving for the gospel and the poor through all this channels iterated above, we shall begin to experience a 'new created and complete life' void of limitations and lack since whatever we give returns back to us in abundance beyond description since there is always a running over, press down shall men and angels commit to your trust.

CHAPTER FIVE
EXAMINING THE DYNAMICS OF NEW-BIRTH AS A SURE ELIXIR TO GENEROSITY

The human life is selfish and covetous in its nature and can never respond to the generous lifestyle of giving, rather the human life only take giving as an investment with God and when it fails, he or she fails to be committed to the habit of giving.

Their kind or manner of giving attitude is conditional and influenced with probabilities. There is no sense or drive of fellowship with God in thanksgiving, kingdom dream, and generosity in their motive of giving but self-centered on what to gain from God or they quit giving.

Such a selfish life-style is the product of the human life and cannot lay their treasures down, since their heart is far from God, though they draw to God with lips in hypocrisy which is the picture of the rich young man in scriptures, when Jesus told him that if he wants to be perfect, let him go and sell everything and come and follow Him, but he went back sad.

"Jesus said unto him, if thou wilt be perfect, go and sell thou hast, and give to the poor, and thou shalt have treasure in heaven: and come and follow me. But when the young man heard that saying, he went away sorrowful: for he had great possessions. Then said Jesus unto his disciples, Verily I say unto you, That a rich man shall hardly enter into the kingdom of heaven" Matt. 19:21-23kjv.

The rich young man went away sorrowful which is the picture of the human unregenerate life that is always sad and sorrowful to give or contribute to just cause but always in the habit of accumulating worldly goods and that is why their soul is never satisfied to have enough.

Jesus offered him the secret of possessing rest in life when one's life is not entangles or engrossed with worldly vanities, though he or she possesses all things, but the young man went away offended because of his fear of losing everything which is poverty.

The young man was rich in earthly possession, but so poor in spiritual possessions of rest or peace, abundance, cheerfulness, love and gratitude which only the divine life procured through new-birth in Christ can offer to any thirsty soul that desires to operate in kingdom wealth or economy system.

The wealth or riches of this world is procured through accumulation that have sorrow attached to it since it operates under the curse of man's selfishness, while the true wealth or riches of the kingdom of God is procured through contribution and have no sorrow attached to it since it operates under the blessing of God's abundance. "The blessing of the LORD, it maketh rich, and he addeth no sorrow with it." Prov. 10:22kjv.

Anyone that is truly born of God through new-birth experience is always delightsome in the attitude of giving as a lifestyle not out of compulsion, but generous in him or her approach of giving which becomes a sure elixir of generosity.

Let us jointly examine in brief the exegesis of the concept of the new-birth experience which is an extract from my book 'experiencing the supernatural' that can turn any mortal man to immortal thereby responding to the attitude of generosity in operating in kingdom wealth and prosperity in this last days which is the dream of God for all mortals in distributing His economy system of abundance on the earth in satisfying His just cause in order to terminate the Babylonian systems of lack and selfishness whereupon money being the only driver.

THE EXCLUSIVE CONCEPT OF NEW-BIRTH

A concept is an understanding retained in the mind, from either experience, reasoning and/or imagination. In this chapter, join me to explore the whole or entire understanding of new birth which will be the major foundation of operating in the supernatural and also a sure elixir to the life of generosity.

New-birth experience is sometimes strange, repugnant and impossible for religious folks due to their natural, philosophical or sensual approach to the whole concept of the work of salvation.

When Nicodemus a religious Jewish teacher or Rabi met Jesus, desiring to experience the supernatural, due to his close observance in the works and words of Jesus, which was so amazing, fascinating and far above the religion that he found himself; he was even one of the Jewish mentor.

The Lord Jesus told him a simple truth and is the only truth that the whole human race need to hear, accept and experience which is the only antidote or answer to man's greatest quest and search for; (1). Significance or value (what is my worth?), (2). The quest and search for destiny (where am I heading to?) (3). Potential (what am I capable of doing to affect lives or make a meaning or what am I here for?), (4). Origin, (where am I coming from?) And (5) Identity (whom am I?).

This five-fold dilemma can never be solved or given answer to by our natural senses or philosophies or school systems, but by tapping into another realm of life; the supernatural!

As a matter of fact our school systems are built around men's philosophies, ideologies, hypothesis, natural laws or natural senses to solve this five-fold dilemma in every man's life which has led into the multiplicity of courses that we offer in schools and also the several kinds of disciplines in our societies to run our economy systems but hadn't given man the answer for satisfaction, value, peace, hope, security, prosperity, abundance and love; rather, it had left man into the oblivion of injustice, fear, hate, jealousy, murder, selfishness, lack, competition and quest for power to dominate others.

What a confused state of man without the new-birth into the supernatural or kingdom realm of life which is also the sure elixir the life of generosity and abundance in operating the kingdom wealth and prosperity on the earth!

Going by scriptures, in John 3:1-6 kjv.) "THERE WAS a man of the Pharisees, named Nicodemus, a ruler of the Jews: The same came to Jesus by night, and said unto him, Rabbi, we know that thou art a teacher come from God: for no man can do these miracles that thou doest, except God be with him. Jesus answered and said unto him, Verily, verily, I say unto thee, Except a man be born again, he cannot see the kingdom of God. Nicodemus saith unto him, How can a man be born when he is old? Can he enter the second time into his mother's womb, and be born? Jesus answered, Verily, verily, I say unto thee, Except a man be born of water and of spirit, he cannot enter into the kingdom of God. That which is born of the flesh is flesh; and that which is born of the Spirit is spirit"

This verse is a graphic illustration on how to be born into the supernatural or the kingdom of God to solve or answer the whole dilemma and quest for any man for satisfaction, love, security, destiny, abundance, peace and value etc. Before going into details on how can a man be born again, Nicodemus asked Jesus that; "can a man be born again when he is old and can he enter the second time into his mother's womb, and be born?"

The simple answer to this question is that, it is not a natural birth but supernatural by the agency of the Spirit and the Word of God which will be discussed on how this happens in our human spirit.

Jesus told Nicodemus twice that if he is not born again, he will neither see (meaning that he will not be able to **understand** the working principles of the kingdom or the supernatural life) nor enter (meaning he will not be able to **experience** the kingdom life or the supernatural here on earth), which implies that except one is born of the Spirit (to experience) or the word of God (to understand), he or she cannot understand or experience the supernatural or the new- birth reality, very important.

The reason why it is termed 'born again' as iterated by the Lord Jesus is because you were born first naturally through flesh and blood into this earth to experience the affairs of this natural and human life which was death, since we all died in the first Adam, but you ought to be born again or anew by another dimension of birth, called new-birth (new in a sense that this kind or pattern of birth had not existed before) through the Spirit and the Word into the kingdom of God in order to experience the affairs of the supernatural or God kind of life on earth.

This further entails that just as the man's sperm will mix with the woman's egg in the womb of the woman with the process called **fertilization** to produce natural babies known as human being, the same thing occur in the realm of the spirit when God's Word and Spirit are mixed together in the womb of our heart or spirit with the process called **believe and confession** to form spiritual babies known as God being that is free from selfishness, lack and sorrows.

The natural baby that is born through sperm and eggs is known as human being i.e. living soul having the character threats or DNA of Man, and the supernatural baby that is born through Spirit and Word is known as God-being i.e. quickening Spirit having the character threats or DNA of God (describing by contrast).

As scriptures says; 'when the perfect comes, it is replaced with the imperfect', which depicts that the moment an individual is born of the Word and Spirit, even though he or she was born natural before, they shall be a complete exchange of the life of God flooding through our human or natural life in order to operate as God in all dimensions. "…that you may be filled [through all your being] unto all the fullness of God [may have the richest measure of the divine Presence, and become a body wholly filled and flooded with God Himself]" Eph. 3:19b amp.

This has been the intension or plan of God for every man to be flooded with His life in our mortal being in order to change us into immortals or supernatural men even while in our mortal bodies for the reason of directing and controlling earthly affairs just as He does in heaven."For God, who commanded the light to shine out of darkness, hath shined in our hearts, to give the light of the knowledge of the glory of God in the face of Jesus Christ. But we have this treasure in earthen vessels, that the excellency of the power may be of God, and not of us" kjv.

I discovered recently that whoever that is not born of the Spirit and Word will be held bound by religious practices or observances or men trying to find the supernatural life.

Religion is the absence of the experiential interactions of the Word and Spirit in our human spirit. The moment one experinces or is born of the Word and Spirit of God, he or she becomes handicapped to religious influences, incapable of performing all its rites, duties and rituals since the soul now has found complete satisfaction and rest in the saving power of grace and truth or Spirit and Word see John 1:17.

HOW TO BE BORN OF THE WORD

The moment one accept or believe that all that Jesus did i.e. his suffering, death and resurrection was done for our sake or on our behalf, and goes further to confess Him as Lord with the mouth and believe with the heart that God raised Him from the death for our righteousness, justification, wisdom, sanctification

and redemption, see 1st Cor. 1:30, you are immediately born of the Word and counted as righteous with evidence of righteousness, peace and joy showing in that person's life; because you believe you are sanctified i.e. separated from being controlled by the earthly corrupt way of life or thinking into the kingdom pure way of life.

Believing with the heart that God raised Jesus from the death leads unto righteousness while confessing Him with your mouth as Lord leads one unto salvation—which becomes the whole package of redemption or why Christ died; for peace, joy, prosperity, righteousness, health eternal life etc.

It is a matter of belief, trusting or accepting and confessing the Lord Jesus and you are born by the Word. Don't figure out how it takes place in our human spirits but just do your part of believing and confessing just as a man and woman does their part and don't know how and when the baby is formed in the womb.

HOW TO BE BORN OF THE SPIRIT

When a natural baby is born into the earthly world, the parents begin to desire on how to train or educate that child in school in order to get him or her acquainted with the earthly economy system of geography, commerce, politics, socials etc. by going through a formation or school, which is another word for been born through that system; because another version of you emerges, since there is a change of thoughts, feelings and psychology or reason, there is definitely a change of life, and any formation or school is the change of one' thoughts and life into a newer version. The quality of our thoughts is the quality of our life. Schools are where thoughts are formed, trained or upgraded into a newer version or quality for more relevance in our world.

In the same way, when one is born of the Word, he or she becomes a supernatural baby in the kingdom of God but needs to be educated, now, not in our physical school system but in the school of the Spirit of God in order to be enlightened and relevant about the economy system of heaven.

As a matter of facts, no matter how bouncing or beautiful a natural baby may look like, without going through school, which is the same as the supernatural baby been born through the school of the Spirit, their relevance will never be seen, rather, he or she become a waste or liability either on earth or the kingdom of God. You should know that our dual or hypostatic nature could permit us to operate heaven or the kingdom life here on earth as it is done in heaven after been schooled or born by the Holy Spirit for relevance as immigrants from the kingdom of heaven to operate the same kingdom government system here on earth.

This analogy also implies on those who are born of the Word, no matter how religious you may be, without being born of the Spirit, you cannot be of relevance in the kingdom of God nor enjoy God on earth, which most Christians are facing today been bored by religious rituals without experiencing God by not been born of the Spirit and still looking for meaning, power, destiny which the Spirit reveals to those who are born of Him. "Now we have received, not the spirit of the world, but the spirit which is of God; that we might know the things that are given freely to us of God"

1st Cor. 2:12kjv and also in 1st John 2:27kjv says; "But the anointing which ye have received of him abideth in you, and ye need not that any man teach you: but as the same anointing teacheth you of all things, and is truth, and no lie, and even as it hath taught you, ye shall abide in him".

We discussed previously that one is born of the Word when we **belief or trust** and **confess** the Lord Jesus, but one is born of the Spirit through DESIRE i.e. desiring the indwelling and infilling of the Holy-Spirit even as the earthly parents desires education for their children or the children desire education for themselves when they have come of age.

The body of Christ has come of age to be born or fully schooled in the Spirit in order to experience the supernatural which is our manifestation here on earth and be exposed to the life of generosity in operating in kingdom wealth in this last days in driving its economy system of abundance, that the whole creation is waiting for to be free from its decadence; "FOLLOW AFTER charity, and **desire spiritual gifts**, but that ye may prophecy" 1st Cor.14:1kjv.(emphasis mine).

THE INTERRACTION BETWEEN THE SPIRIT AND THE WORD.

Theologically and even biblically, we understand that they are three personalities in one God, which is true and I am going to prove it shortly relating to our new-birth of the Word and Spirit. "For there are three that bear record in heaven, the Father, the Word, and the Holy Ghost: and these three are one. And there are three that bear witness in earth, the spirit, and the water, and the blood: and these three agree in one" 1st John 5:7-8kjv.

The verse above graphically presents the interaction between the Spirit and the Word which will be illustrated accordingly. God is a Spirit (see John 4:24), and He is the father, but functions through two component personalities i.e. the Holy-Spirit who represents the body make-up of God in the spiritual realm in carrying out tangibly the activities of God both in the physical and spiritual realm and the Word which represents the soul aspect or component of God comprising of His mind, will and emotion.

That is why when Jesus who is the Word or soul aspect of God wept; many heretics say; does God cry? Yes I will say, because He has a component within His soul [Word] that is emotional i.e. feelings. God is emotional too, and most times feels what we feel. "For we have not an high priest which cannot be touched with the feelings of our infirmities; but was in all points tempted like as we are, yet without sin." Heb. 4:15kjv.

When scriptures says these three bear witness with one another and they are one, it implies that just as in the makeup of man, we are spirit being that possess a soul and housed in a clay body (natural man), comparatively, in the aspect of God, He is a Spirit that possess a Soul [the Word] and is housed or lives in a body [the Holy-Spirit] in carrying out His tangible or visible and invisible activities.

When a man has no clay body, no matter what you think in your mind and approve in your spirit or in yourself, it can never be implemented physically without your clay body. In similarity, no matter how God could plan a thing in His mind [the Word], and approve it in Himself [the Spirit] without the Holy Spirit [His body] it can never be executed visibly either in the spiritual or visible realms or worlds.

The Holy Spirit is the only Spirit that has the capacity and legacy to operate both in the invisible and visible worlds in His single form at the same time; other spirits are restricted including God Himself as a Spirit to operate only in the spiritual realm, unless invited or permitted to use any visible channel, but man is the only spirit that can function both in the invisible and visible worlds, but in this case as hypostatic or double form or nature i.e. with our spirit in the invisible and our clay body in the visible world.

God who is a Spirit cannot operate on earth visibly except by the Holy Spirit or through the human body and demons or devil has no right to operate on earth nor any of the planets except we permit him through our bodies when our minds are captured through his negative or lying information and fear, the same happens with other creatures in other planets.

Among all creatures, even in other planets, God choose only man to dwell in and to share his complete image and likeness—His fullness; others are all in part, but we men are complete in Him, see Col. 2:10. It is a mystery that cannot be digested in this book.

The moment we are born of the Word and Spirit interactively, we become as God, operating in the same measure of strength, power, riches, honor, authority, wisdom, blessings and glory as in God with only one difference which is to acknowledge Him as Lord and worship Him by giving Him glory.

Going by the same scriptures we read above, 'And there are three that bear witness in earth, the spirit, and the water, and the blood: and these three agree in one'. Man is a spirit, but when he is born of water [which implies the Word] and the blood [which implies the spirit, since the blood incubates the life and the spirit of that being]. That man becomes a new creation or creature i.e. he has not existed before in that kind.

That man now becomes a recreated spirit that possess not just the previous kind of soul, but now the soul of God [His mind, emotion and will or desires] through the continuous transforming power of the Word to make it manifest, since our previous will is involved and God cannot force, impose or manifest His Will into our human will without our permission, so it takes a process on how long or short we allow Him to be completely changed into Him.

"Let this mind be in you, which was also in Christ Jesus." Phil. 2:5kjv. And then we as spirit are housed in our clay body, though as it were not just our physical body exist now alone, but is now enabled or empowered by the body of God; the Holy-Spirit to operate in God's dimension.

God now lives or dwells completely in man through our new birth i.e. our spirit now is regenerated into the Spirit of Jesus and relates directly with the [Spirit of God inside our new or regenerated human spirit (the Spirit of Jesus), then our soul now is transformed into the mind or Word or Soul of God, and finally our body is vitalized or empowered by the Holy Spirit; the body of God, to dwell within as one.

This confirms the scripture in Col. 2:9-10a, Amp. "For in Him the whole fullness of Deity (the Godhead) continues to dwell in bodily form [giving complete expression of the divine nature] And you are in Him, made full and having come to fullness of life [in Christ you too are filled with the Godhead—Father, Son and Holy Spirit— and reach full spiritual stature]." This is exactly what we've been made now in Christ. This is so great and every man has the right to hear! We now live or manifest the complete expression of the divine nature bodily. "As He is in heaven, so are we now on earth" see 1st John 5:17.

Now, in every man that has experienced the new birth, his spirit houses God as a Spirit, his former soul is now changed into the Word or the soul of God and his body temples the Holy Spirit. "Know ye not that ye are the temple of God, and that the Spirit of God dwelleth in you? 1st Cor, 3:16.

This verse was referring to our spirit man that houses God as a Spirit; that our spirit now is the house of God as Spirit and we should avoid the sin of the spirit which are; envy, strive, division etc. It is different from 1st Cor. 6:19 "What? Know ye not that your body is the temple of the Holy Ghost which is in you, which ye have of God, and ye are not your own?

This verse refers to your human body as the temple of the Holy-Spirit (the body of God) given to you by God to dwell in your mortal body in order for God to think his thought through you, carry out His activities through your mortal body known as the gift of the Spirit or natural talents as though He was the one physically present, and that we should avoid the sin of the flesh, which is fornication since the Holy-Spirit (God's body) is living now directly in our clay bodies, what a divine honor!

Most theologians and philosophers don't actually know the differences between the Holy Spirit and God as a Spirit, so you've known now that God is Spirit that dwells in our human spirit and the Holy Spirit is the body aspect or manifest presence of God that dwells in our clay bodies by empowering it in carrying out the plan of God which is His mind or Word and has become ours via transformation of our mind or soul as though He is the one Physically present.

The new man now has God as a Spirit in his human spirit, has the Word [the soul aspect of God] in his soul being changed to be as God's Soul as we behold Him daily in worship and His Word

see 2nd Cor. 3:18 , then our body now houses the Body of God [the Holy-Spirit]. "But if the Spirit of him that raised up Jesus from the dead dwell in you [**the body**], he that raised up Christ from the dead shall also quicken your mortal bodies by his Spirit that dwelleth in you [**the body**]" Rom.8:11. Emphases added.

God now physically dwells in man [the new-birth or born again man] with His Spirit in our human spirits, his Soul [mind, will and emotion] in our soul and His Body as the Holy Spirit in our clay body in order for man to experience and operate the supernatural, eternal or God kind of life, the fullness of God now on earth naturally that is generous in nature.

The moment any man be in Christ or is born of the Word and Spirit interactively, the kind of life that exudes out from that man is called eternal life. This life is not to be experienced in heaven only as taught by religion but rather it is a kind of life that should be experienced here and now on earth, since the new created or born again man has it now. "He that hath the Son hath life; and he that hath not the Son of God hath not life. These things have I written unto you that believe on the name of the Son of God; that ye may know that ye have eternal life, and that ye may believe on the name of the Son of God." 1st John 5:12-13kjv. We have six kinds of life which are; [A]. The Earth life. [B]. Plant life [C]. Animal life, [D]. Human life, [E]. Angelic life and [F]. The God life.

Mankind was redeemed not with earth, plant, animal, human or angel life which would have ended up having any of these qualities or class of life. But we were redeemed or bought back with the life of God in the person of His Son Jesus, so that we could have or share in the same class or pattern or quality of God's life bodily which is the highest kind of life, we mortals now have been given privilege by God to have access into eternal or God kind of life as though it were ours that even angels desire to look into this wonders, see 1st Pet. 1:11-12 & 18-19.

Eternal life is not just everlasting life that will be lived in the gold streets of heaven by and by which is free from death, sickness, pain etc. but rather, though everlasting, it is a quality or kind of life which is the very life of God that we mortals have been given the license and access to live here and now on earth as God does in heaven to conquer, and gain control over the elements of this life and remain comfortable or occupy till Jesus returns, thereby enforcing naturally the will or kingdom of God on earth as it is done in heaven, see Luke 19:13 & 11:2.

This life we've been given access to, is far more that the angelic life and attracts their honor on our person which was not so in the Old Testament when we were lower than angels after the fall of Adam and a bit lower than God before the fall, but now we are exactly as God after the redemption that Jesus wrought for mankind at the cross. This is good news!

Let me graphically illustrate what happens when one accept Jesus as Lord into his or her life by using some scriptures as shown to me in experiencing eternal life or God kind of Life or the supernatural now on earth, before concluding on this chapter.

One certain day the Lord told me that the gospel is all about telling men and women that they now have complete right to advance or upgrade their lives from their natural human weak life subject to temptations, selfishness, lack, fear, sin, death, poverty, sickness into God kind of life [the supernatural or eternal life] that is superior to sickness, poverty, sin, temptations, lack, selfishness, weakness, death etc.

He said that, if I could do that, I have been able to preach the whole truth that Jesus preached and even died for, which is simply the gospel of grace, and the Gospel of grace is all about experiencing immortality and the God kind of life on earth naturally "But is now made manifest by the appearing of our Saviour Jesus Christ, who hath abolished death, and hath brought life and immortality to light through the gospel. see Acts 14:3. Please all ministers of the gospel reading this book should take note of this truth.

The following biblical references validate this point of men and women coming into eternal or supernatural realm of life and making it their own kind of life through faith or consciousness of this truth. "The thief commeth not, but for to steal, and to kill, and to destroy: I am come that they might have life [eternal life], and that they might have it more abundantly" John 10:10 emphases mine., "For I have not spoken of myself; but the Father which sent me, he gave me a commandment, what I should say, and what I should speak. And I know that his commandment is **life everlasting**: whatsoever I speak therefore, even as the Father said unto me, so I speak." John 12:49-50. And " John 17: 2-3, "As thou hast given him power over all flesh, that he should give eternal life to as many as thou hast given him. And this is life eternal, that they might know thee the only true God, and Jesus Christ, whom thou hast sent."

As a matter of emphasis, the amplified rendered John 10:10 as thus; "The thief comes only in order to steal and kill and destroy. I came that they may have and enjoy life, and have it in abundance (to the full, till it overflows). This is great! The purpose why Jesus came was for us mortals to have and enjoy life; God kind or class of life until it overflows to others, thereby establishing the kingdom life of God on earth among others before Jesus returns.

We have been redeemed to have and enjoy God kind of life; by implication, we mortals through new-birth have been called to live a life of pleasure and complete satisfaction and rest, free from sickness, poverty, guilt, sin and fear of the unknown, death, failure and all sorts of mishaps, what a life we have now in Christ!

The moment you are born of God, you have the right to reject any other form of life contrary to the kind of life we've just described, so that the wicked one the devil wouldn't take advantage to deceive you that you don't have what you've already gotten now in Christ via new-birth.

Eternal or God kind or class of life or the supernatural is all about living the life of the father, Son and Holy Spirit now on earth bodily and in the world beyond. Some scriptures were exposed to me recently to buttress more on this truth; that we who are born of the Word and Spirit are now living intrinsically the life of Jesus in 1st Cor. 15:45, "And so it is written, The first man Adam was made a living soul; the last Adam was made a quickening spirit".

The first Adam which is our old nature was made a living soul or 'received life'. God told me that the first Adam was a living or lively soul i.e. Man who is a spirit, with a highly sensitive soul, and housed in a clay body.

The spirit was upright and the soul was so powerful and super sensitive to God but lacked the capacity for God to dwell in; that is why man was a living soul, he was created to operate in his own kind or class of life as a living soul or human life or received life.

Man was ruled more of the mind or soul than the spirit in interacting more into earthly things , since we were living soul, but the new man is ruled or controlled more of the spirit than the mind or soul, since we are now quickened or living spirit or life givers. In the dispensation of the old Adam, man received life to live as living souls, but in the dispensation of the new Adam in the person of Jesus, man now have become a quickening spirit, i.e. a life giver, we are now full of life until it overflows just as God.

God only came and visited man as a Spirit in fellowship and goes back since the quality and capacity of the life of man then was just human and could not retain nor house God permanently, which is why it is a living soul i.e. a small part of God on earth and not the fullness since we were made in His image and likeness.

Now, those who are born of the Word and Spirit in the order of the second Adam' are having now a new spirit man, since the old spirit man died in sin or disobedience, God now quickened the fallen man in His Son Jesus. Quicken means to bring back to life what was or is dead, and in this case, we were not only brought back to life, but were also given the capacity to be givers of life since it now overflows in the order of God.

Our spirit that was dead in the first Adam is now brought back to life by the second Adam—Jesus' since he is the quickening or life-giving spirit. The spirit of man that was dead was not brought back or quickened into our previous state of living soul or human life or spirit which could not accommodate or housed God, rather, it was now quickened into the very life and Spirit of Jesus—the

Word; God's Word is life and spirit see John 6:63.

The Amplified version of the bible iterated this truth in Eph. 2:5. "Even when we were dead (slain) by [our own] shortcomings and trespasses, He made us alive together in fellowship and in union with Christ; [He gave us the very life of Christ Himself, the same new life with which He quickened Him, for] it is by grace (his favor and mercy which you did not deserve) that you are saved (delivered from judgment and made partakers of Christ's salvation."

You see, if anyone be in Christ he is a new creation, old human life passes away, behold the new life of God replaces that old one in us, which means that such a man ceases to live the old Adam 'living soul life' of sin and disobedience, and now begins to live the 'quickened life' of God in the person of Jesus in the flesh of righteousness and obedience see 2nd Cor.5:17, Rom 5:19. That is why God sees us as Himself or the same way He sees Jesus in our spirit man— as His righteousness.

One scripture was exposed to me recently again about this same truth which turned around my life positively in Rom. 14:17 "For the kingdom of God is not meat and drink; but righteousness, and peace, and joy in the Holy Ghost." We've known by now that the supernatural life is the same with the kingdom life. The verse above declares that those whose life are driven by meat and drink i.e. the natural Adam or living soul class of material conscious life in the absence of God cannot experience the kingdom of God; rather it takes those who have passed through new-birth which is characterized by righteousness, peace and joy in the Holy Ghost to experience the kingdom class of life or the supernatural. Please pay close attention here!

God made us His righteousness in our spirit by new-birth, since God is righteousness in nature. "For he hath made him to be sin for us, who knew no sin; that we might be made the righteousness of God in him". 2nd Cor.5:21. And our soul (comprising of the mind, will and emotion) is now garrisoned with the peace of God who is Jesus—he is the prince of Peace "… and his name shall be called Wonderful, Counsellor, The mighty God, The everlasting Father, The Prince of Peace." Isaiah 9:6bkjv. This verse was talking about Jesus living in our soul-mind now as the Prince of Peace.

Finally, the Holy Spirit that dwell now in our clay or mortal bodies now influences it with joy due to His presence "Thou wilt show me the path of life: in thy presence is fullness of joy;…" Ps. 16:11a, making it complete as in the supernatural or kingdom life lived in us now on earth bodily or naturally, comprising of God the father, Son ,and Holy-Spirit living inside of our spirit, soul and body, and manifesting righteousness through our spirit from the father, peace through our soul from the Son and joy through our body or conscious mind or five-senses from the Holy Spirit which is the manifestation of the kingdom of God as we saw in Rom. 14:17.

We've now been made the righteousness of God in our spirit man, The Peace of Jesus in our soul and the joy of the Holy Spirit in our clay body or conscious mind bodily. Having such an experience is the kingdom of God or the supernatural or the fullness of the stature of Christ. That is the reason why the next verse of Rom. 14:17 declares that "For he that in these things serveth Christ is acceptable to God, and approved of men". This is a perfect kind of life which has been God's dream for everyman. "Be ye therefore perfect, even as your Father which in heaven is perfect". Matt 5:48.

Paul caught this same revelation and iterated it more in some other scriptures as thus; "And because ye are sons, God hath sent forth the Spirit of his Son into your hearts, crying, Abba, Father". Gal. 4:6kjv. This is what most religion will never understand or experience except they accept the new-birth.

God has sent **the Spirit of His Son** which is not different from **the Holy-Spirit** and **God as a Spirit** to replace our human heart or spirit thereby empowering or quickening it in order to be able to accommodate God as Spirit inside of us. It is only the Spirit of Jesus that has the capacity to accommodate or house God as a

Spirit permanently which we now possess via new birth.

The Spirit of Jesus is what we possess in new birth and it now accommodates God intrinsically within our new created spirit; what the first Adam or natural man could never experience or be able to accommodate i.e. the living soul!

We who are born again have the capacity to accommodate God as a Spirit in our new created spirit, being exactly in the class of the Spirit or life of Jesus. Also in Gal. 2:20, St. Paul said, " I am crucified with Christ: nevertheless I live; yet not I, but Christ liveth in me: and the life which I now live in the flesh I live by faith of the Son of God, who loved me, gave himself for me".

All these scriptural truth indicates that when we are born again, our old spirit man or nature which was dead with dark works of sin is replaced with a new spirit of life in Christ, which means that our lives or spirit is now exactly like that of Jesus and not of Adam any longer making us as generous and selfless as God Himself. What a holy exchange!

We are now as rich as Christ, since we are exactly as Him, and Jesus is the treasure house of the fullness of God (i.e. all that God is and has), see Col. 1:19, we also are the treasure house of the fullness of God bodily see John 1:16. And are now complete of made perfect in Him to operate in His dimension, even in the life of generosity and selflessness, Colossians 2:10.

Let's move into the last chapter of this book in understanding and accessing the grace of giving which we already possess now by new-birth experience in order to operate maximally in kingdom wealth and prosperity on earth, so interesting!

CHAPTER SIX

CRAVING FOR THE EMPOWERMENT
OF THE GIVING GRACE

In the kingdom economy system of wealth, before one could have power to receive, they must be a corresponding power to lay down something, the motivation or empowerment to receiving is in the joy of giving.

God empowers us to get "But thou shalt remember the LORD thy God: for it is he that giveth thee power to get wealth, that he may establish his covenant which he sware unto thy fathers, as it is this day" Deut.8:18kjv. God empowers us to get rich and it is expedient to remember Him in our generous giving as a sense of worship, thankfulness and appreciation for His benevolence and bountifulness towards us.

But it takes the giving grace to always remember the Lord or be empowered to lay down that which we've gotten from God. Cain and Abel brought an offering before God, but the one of Cain was rejected because he did not offer it well as the best of his first fruit but gave out of convenience, necessity and burden but Abel brought cheerfully the firstlings of his flock and of the fat also displaying the gravity of honour attached to his giving to God which was powerful. See Gen. 4:3ff.

Let us take a close look at the Macedonia church in 2nd Cor. 8:1-3 "MOREOVER, brethren, we do you to wit of the grace of God bestowed on the churches of Mac-e-do'ni-a; How that in a great trial of affliction the abundance of their joy and their deep poverty abounded unto the riches of their liberality. For to their power,

I bear record, yea, and beyond their power they were willing of themselves;"

Their worth of liberality was even recognized by Paul as a reference point when he was addressing the Philippians church, "Now ye Philippians know also, that in the beginning of the gospels, when I departed from Macedonia, no church communicated with me as concerning giving and receiving, but ye only" Phil. 4:15kjv.

It took only the grace of giving in the Macedonia church that in the midst of their poor economic situation, they still gave generously with utmost joy even beyond their capacity and by that act, they had access into the abundance of God even in their deep poverty.

This attitude of giving must be our desire to be empowered with the giving grace that violates all manner of economic situations and circumstances in determining our motive of giving. This Macedonia church in their deep poverty notwithstanding gave beyond their power out of joy and not sorrow of heart since they were empowered to do so.

The life or attitude of generous and joyful giving is a realm or dimension where God operates His abundance and when we come in contact with that realm or grace or life of God, giving become inexcusable, inexhaustible and unexplainable but done with great delight.

The children of Israel gave willing in the construction of their temple of worship as shown to Moses to a point that he started rejecting their offerings since it was more than enough for the completion of the task. "The children of Israel brought a willing offering unto the LORD, every man and woman, whose heart made them willing to bring for all manner of work, which the LORD had commanded to be made by the hand of Moses." Exo. 35:29kjv.

This act of willingness was perfected in the thirty sixth chapters of Exodus from verse five to six. "And they spake unto Moses, saying, The people bring much more than enough for the service of the work, which the LORD commanded to make. And Moses gave commandment, and they caused it to be proclaimed throughout the camp, saying, Let neither man nor woman make any more work for the offering of the sanctuary. So the people were restrained from bringing. For the stuff they had was sufficient for all the work to make it, and too much."

This attitude of giving displayed by the children of Israel is not human or natural but it was empowered by the giving grace which enabled them to give more than enough for the completion of the sanctuary.

We need such a supernatural empowerment to even give beyond our power or human best such that one could always have access into the over flowing or running over blessing, both spiritual and earthly since we can never out-give God, they is always a mega reward system that flows to willing and cheerful givers since God Loves them.

Let's take a close look at Luke's gospel 6:38 in exploring the seven dimension of the return of blessing whether in kind, conduct or cash, investment of time, talent and treasure on righteous cause when the life of giving willingly is activated. "give, and it shall be given unto you; good measure, pressed down, and shaken together, and running over, shall men give to your bosom. For with the same measure that ye mete withal it shall be measured to you again."

These seven dimensions of return of a giver in every ramification are; A. it shall be given unto you back on the basis on whatever you give. B. It shall be a return of good measure. C. it shall be a pressed down return, in other words a compressed blessing. D. It shall also be a return of shaken together blessing as in expanded blessing to accommodate more. E. it shall be a return of running over or overflow blessing which makes such folk to be a channel of blessing to others. F. it shall be a return of men being compelled to stock your store houses and bags with what you gave out and

G. The gravity of the returned blessing shall be concomitant with the measure, quantity and quality of what you gave out in the first instance which shall come back to you in that magnitude exponentially.

When I understood this Luke 6:38 principle of giving I came to a conclusion that givers never lack and 'lackers' never give and immediately the fear of giving left me immediately which is poverty and it simultaneously injected in me the grace and gratitude of giving that have connected me to abundance and the power to receive good things or favour with good understanding both in the sight of men and God. "Let not mercy and truth forsake thee: bind them about thy neck; write them upon the table of thine heart: So shalt thou find favour and good understanding in the sight of God and man." Pro. 3:3-4kjv.

Mercy and truth are elixirs of a generous lifestyle and the foundation of the giving grace whereupon it naturally attracts favour and good understanding in the sight of God and men which inoculates you from all sorts of lack and wants by granting you major access to God's benevolence, bounties or abundance which is His will for all His children in this last days, to show the world through us how much of His wealth and riches He has bestowed in us.

CONCLUSION

God's intension for the last day's church is to prosper us spiritually as in our faith power, materially as in our finances and possessions even as our soul prospers emotionally. "Beloved, I wish above all things that thou mayest prosper and be in health, even as thy soul prospers" 3rd John vs.2.

One of the agenda's of God for the end-time church is to daze us His sons and daughters with His wealth and riches for the purpose of furthering His righteous cause of establishing His kingdom here on earth through the preaching of the gospel and the help of the needy.

Since one of the strongest distraction to any natural soul from response to the eternal salvation of God through the gospel is the pursuit for material things even in the expense of their salvation due to fear of the unknown, mostly the fear of not meeting up to the demands of this life.

Men and women could be sold out into several kinds of low hideous choices on how to live their lives or make ends meet and neglect the ultimate choice of their service to God in Christ which becomes one of the challenges of driving the gospel of the kingdom across the face of the earth. Even in the time of Jesus Christ in His gospel campaign, He fed the hungry which is one of the basic need or necessity of humanity.

The last days church need to be buoyant materially since this selfish world system of only accumulating things don't even care how much you know, but want to know how much you care even after sharing with them the righteousness, peace and joy of the kingdom, they desire to experience it materially, mostly when they are poor nations or people in giving them the picture of how much God is ready to cater for their need having loved them in dying at the cross for their sins.

Let me share an extract from my book, 'The six point agenda of God for the end-time church' on this note, such that you could be positioned through the information iterated in this book to be one of the sons or daughter of God that will be chosen or dignified to lavish His wealth and riches through to this passing world.

'Due to the operation of divine life at work in every believer, it begins to produce divine wisdom, discipline and creative work in the body of Christ in these last days, which enhances our viability, credibility and ability as solution givers to nations.

Thereupon, they shall begin to run or flow to us for help, whereupon the body of Christ, the church will be immersed with the wealth of nations and honor that have never and ever shall be experienced before the rapture of the saints or the end of this world.

Remember that through prosperity shall the gospel be carried globally. "Cry yet, saying, Thus saith the Lord of hosts; My cities through prosperity shall yet be spread abroad; and the Lord shall yet comfort Zion, and shall choose Jerusalem" Zech. 1:17kjv.

"But in the last days it shall come to pass, that the mountain of the house of the Lord shall be established in the top of the mountains, and it shall be exalted above the hills; and people shall flow unto it. And many nations shall come, and say, come, and let us go up to the mountain of the Lord, and to the house of the God of Jacob; and he will teach us of his ways, and we will walk in his paths: for the law shall go forth of Zion and the word of the Lord from Jerusalem." Micah 4:1-2.

Hermeneutically and eschatological point of view, this passage could be referred to the millennium reign of Christ, but as I said earlier that all these last days events are so interwoven that they overlap each other, it eluded and robbed the mechanics of time, space and matter. But as it where, the mount Zion stands for the spiritual mount Zion; which is the church, the body of Christ. "But ye are come unto mount Sion, and unto the city of the living God, the heavenly Jerusalem, and to an innumerable company of angels, To the general assembly and church of firstborn, which are written in heaven, and to God the judge of all, and to the spirits of just men made perfect, and to Jesus the mediator of the new covenant, and to the blood of sprinkling, that speaketh better things than that of Abel." Heb. 12:22-24.

The beauty of the church in this last days will be so attractive that even the unbelievers and other religious sect shall begin to find their way to the church and ask us the way out and the way forward of all their search and endeavors, and we the church shall give them answers because eternal life is fully at work now in us and we can now demonstrate the omnipotence, omniscient and omnipresence nature of God naturally through us to this helpless world.

In this last days, the philosophy and educational system shall fail which is already happening, since it cannot meet the contentions of the dark world, right now as I speak, the wicked one have began to render to foolishness the wisdoms and intelligence of this world or natural men, to the extent that most predictions of our scientific discoveries are no more coming through again or functional as it use to be, all because of the cultic powers of darkness and dark powers of the air working so hard to rule this world, but thanks be to God that we the church are the light of the world to scatter all their machinations in every strata of human endeavor and procuring eternal solutions to this helpless world, through the wisdom and power of God at work in us, which is our arsenal against the onslaughts of hell in this last days.

The book of Isaiah actually gave a clearer rendition of the church as solution givers to teach this passing world addressing every strata of human endeavors starting from salvation, since their philosophies and theologies failed, we the church becomes the mountain of solution to other mountains and hills of men's ideologies. "And it shall come to pass in the last days, that the mountain of the Lord's house shall be established in the top of the mountains, and shall be exalted above the hill; and all nations shall flow unto it. And many people shall go and say, Come ye, and let us go up to the mountain of the Lord, to the house of the God of Jacob; and he will teach us of his ways, and we will walk in his paths; for out of Zion shall go forth the law, and the word of the Lord from Jerusalem." Isa. 2:2-3kjv.

Now, let's be more practical, in this world today, men that matters much and had rebranded this world are those with talents and skills and not just certificates and grades carriers. God in this last day is anointing His sons and daughters with divine talents and skills that the world has never known, heard or seen in addressing every stratum of human endeavors and needs whereupon attracting all the dignities, honor and wealth of nations into the body of Christ just as what happened to the children of Israel when departing the land of Egypt since this are also the days of departure or exodus of the glorious church.

We shall win favors from the world systems as never before thereby gathering the wealth of nations back to the body of Christ for the purpose of our outreaches both in the gospel and meeting their natural needs, causing a global evangelism and revival to every nook and cranny of the earth, touching the unsaved of about four billion souls that have not heard the gospel before the rapture since God intends that no soul be lost, but all should come into repentance, and the only way to get them saved is through the preaching of the gospel. "The Lord is not slack concerning his promise, as some men count slackness; but is longsuffering to us-ward, not willing that any should perish, but that all should come to repentance" 2nd Pet 3:9kjv.

Have this in mind that we are in the last days, and in these days as I have said, God is rising up financial giants in the body of Christ. Now, listen to this; God is not releasing His wealth to strangers, who do not care to know nor love Him and His ultimate purpose of saving lost souls and catering for the needs of the poor, but God is releasing His wealth to His loved sons and daughters in order to enhance His kingdom assignment of souls on the earth.

God is all out to empower His people for supernatural wealth and riches in these last days, so they can become channels for the release of His silver, ordained for building the latter house in its glory which house is you and all saved souls.

"And I will shake all nations, and the desire of all nations shall come: and I will fill this house with glory, saith the Lord of host. The silver is mine, and the gold is mine, saith the Lord of hosts. The glory of this latter house shall be greater than of the former, saith the Lord of hosts: and in this place will I give peace, saith the Lord of hosts" Hag. 2:7-9kjv. God is taking His wealth back to His church to be run by His sons and daughters for His ultimate purpose of souls rescue which we all have been called to herald in this end times.

Remember that in Zechariah 1:17 "Cry yet, saying, Thus saith the Lord of host; My cities through prosperity shall yet be spread abroad; and the Lord shall yet comfort Zion, and shall yet choose Jerusalem" Get yourself positioned for your dignity and honor to be restored supernaturally, as you become a willing and cheerful kingdom addicted giver and helper to the poor and God' prophets and ministers of the gospel.

How much we are willing to give out towards kingdom advancement is what determine how much we can be trusted and entrusted with kingdom wealth, because to whom much is given, much is required, "If therefore ye have not been faithful in the unrighteous mammon, who will commit to your trust the true riches" Luke. 16:11.

It was in the heart of David to build God a house and God gave him the resources to build in his hands, that almost all the resources was provided by David. 1ˢᵗ Kings 8:17.

God finally in this last days is showing His kindness or jewels to His sons and daughters as the Father shows kindness to their children that obey or belief them, such that they will be a differences between we the children of light and the children of darkness, they shall be a clear cut different between the righteous and sinners in this last days and by this information in this chapter of being a generous giver from your tithing not as a law but worship to God, offerings and sacrificial giving, the sky is your starting point to the kingdom of wealth which the Father is intending and eager to unleash on His children for His soul rescue agenda in this end-time and now is the appointed time.

"When the Lord shall build up Zion, he shall appear in his glory" so let us "Arise, and shine; for thy light has come, and the glory of the Lord is risen upon thee. For, behold, the darkness shall cover the earth, and gross darkness the people: but the Lord shall arise upon thee, and his glory shall be seen upon thee. And the gentiles shall come to thy light, and kings to the brightness of thy rising" Psalm 102:13&Isa. 60:1-3kjv.

Your light is your knowledge or revelation about certain facts and truth that the world could never fathom or have access to and you shall be the solution whereupon kings shall come to that brightness, then God shall appear in glory after we've come into this dimension of maturity to rapture His glorious church.

"And they shall be mine, saith the Lord of hosts, in that day when I make up [jewels; and I will spare them, as a man spareth his own son that serveth him. Then shall ye return, and discern between the righteous and the wicked, between him that serveth God and that serveth him not" Mal.3:17-18kjv.

It's time to get started in this kingdom mission as evangelizers and become part of these kingdom emissaries on the earth to be a show piece of how wealthy and rich God is to this impoverished and passing world. It's as urgent as we shoulder this responsibility!'

ABOUT THE BOOK

This book have been divinely orchestrated in equipping all believers in Christ and folks that are yet to join the Christian fold in properly positioning them through the expository information in form of epistles and chapters to be enlightened enough in becoming distributors of the wealth and riches of the kingdom of God on the earth.

In this book you will discover among others;

- The basics of kingdom prosperity
- Major channels of distributing kingdom wealth and riches
- How to conquer greed
- Understanding the empowerment of the grace of giving and lots more.

Get this book in order to be enlisted and aligned properly for the possession and distribution of kingdom wealth and prosperity that God is set to lavish through all His sons and daughters on the earth before the coming kingdom age or the rapture and the millennium reign of Christ on the earth.

ABOUT THE AUTHOR

He is an exemplified leader and writer of both motivational and spiritual books. He facilitates seminars in government, companies and business enterprises on work ethics, moral ethics and personnel empowerment. He is also commissioned in hosting revivals, retreats and crusades with a passionate interest to rescue souls from the grip of Satan and sin. He is the author of 'Exploring the Mystery of Faith,' 'Living Above failures', 'Strategy of Overcoming Satanic Plots. 'The Uniqueness in Ladies' etc. He is based in Nigeria and Presides over 'Kingdom Age Assembly' Calabar, Cross River State Nigeria. For counseling and prayers; contact +23408030754420, +23409070024208 or email; Josephmonshumministries@gmail.com.